ISBN-13: 978-0-692-06979-0

This book can be found at www.Amazon.com or by contacting the author at: docroegrandson@gmail.com

Dedicated to the "angel" I knew as "Paw Paw."

First printing: February 2018

HOW EASY COMPANY BECAME A BAND OF BROTHERS

By Chris Langlois, a Doc Roe grandson

Illustrated by Anneke Helleman

"From this day to the ending of the world,
But we in it shall be remembered -
We few, we happy few, we band of brothers;
For he today that sheds his blood with me
Shall be my brother."
- William Shakespeare, *Henry V*

"Where is the prince who can afford so, to cover his country with troops for its defense, so that ten thousand men descending from the clouds might not, in many places, do an infinite deal of mischief before a force could be brought together to repel them?"

- Benjamin Franklin, 1784

"The 101st Airborne Division has no history...but it has a rendezvous with destiny."
- General William C. Lee, 'father' of United States Airborne

"Hang Tough"
Major Dick Winters

101ST AIRBORNE DIVISION (12,000 MEN)

|

506TH PARACHUTE INFANTRY REGIMENT (1,800 MEN)

|

2ND BATTALION (600 MEN)

|

EASY COMPANY (160 MEN)

|

PLATOON (48 MEN)

|

SQUAD (16 MEN)

Airborne Beginnings

The United States airborne program began with an all-volunteer test platoon in July 1940, and it was comprised of two officers and 48 enlisted men. Other countries such as Japan, Italy, Germany, and the Soviet Union already had airborne units. During World War II (WWII), the Germans would conduct two major paratrooper jumps, one in Crete and one in Holland.

The paratrooper concept was still brand new for the United States in 1942 when the 509th Parachute Infantry Battalion took part in the United States' first combat jump in North Africa during *Operation Torch*.

Parachute troops are specially trained, equipped and organized for completing missions that other troops cannot do, such as:

- Seizing terrain only accessible by parachute,
- Seizing river and canal crossings,
- Attacking terrain behind enemy lines in coordinated attacks by other ground and/or naval operations,
- Seizing landing fields for friendly use or to deny use to enemy aircraft,
- Creating confusion and acting as a diversion for the operations of the main force.

On August 16, 1942, the 101st Airborne Division was activated at Camp Claiborne, Louisiana where General William Lee gave his famous speech, "The 101st Airborne Division has no history...but it has a rendezvous with destiny."

The 506th Parachute Infantry Regiment (PIR) was unique for the United States Army in that for the first time, troops would complete basic training and jump school together, thus forming a tighter bond and a more formidable fighting unit. The 506th was activated on July 20, 1942, under the command of West Point graduate Lieutenant Colonel Robert F. Sink and began training at Camp Toccoa, Georgia. Col. Sink would remain the 506th commander until the end of the war, a rare occurrence for an infantry regiment in combat.

Nine rifle companies comprised the 506th: *Able, Baker, Charlie, Dog, Easy, Fox, George, How and Item*. The companies would also be referred to by their first letter, such as E Company.

The 506th's motto became, "Currahee" which translated from the Cherokee language as, "Stands Alone." It was a description of Mount Currahee that dominated the landscape around Camp Toccoa. But it also became the mindset of every paratrooper since they landed behind enemy lines, always surrounded by the enemy and often alone.

Many aspired to be a paratrooper as it paid an extra $50 a month for an enlisted man ($100 a month for officers). That $50 in 1942 would be worth about $800 today. Others sought the adventure of jumping out of airplanes or felt the desire to be their best and be around others in an elite unit who believed the same. Over 500 officers would volunteer, but only 150 completed the training while 5,800 enlisted men signed up with just 1,800 making the grade to be in the regiment.

On June 10, 1943, Easy Company and the rest of the 506th Parachute Infantry Regiment became a part of the 101st Airborne...beginning their own rendezvous with destiny.

RUNNING CURRAHEE

Colonel Sink wanted the 506th to be the best soldiers in the Army. His "boys" would be known as the "Five-0-Sink." Physical training was a sure way to find the cream of the crop. The men of the 506th at Camp Toccoa soon became very familiar with the steep and rocky path up and down Mount Currahee, which rises to almost 1,000 feet.

As the men arrived at Camp Toccoa, they were assigned to tents, lined up in neat rows in the shadow of Mount Currahee. In addition to battling the heat, humidity, ticks and mosquitoes, they were subjected to intense physical demands, including runs up the mountain, sometimes twice a day — three miles up. If a man fell out of the run due to an injury or exhaustion, no one was allowed to help; there was an ambulance waiting. There was no time to admire the view at the top — 3 miles down. Completion in 50 minutes was required. The record was 42 minutes. All the officers ran the mountain; everyone was treated the same in that regard. Those who could not run Currahee were expelled from paratrooper training.

Camp Toccoa also introduced the men to the basics of being an infantry soldier: marching in formation, standing at attention, holding a rifle, using a map and compass, learning attack and defense tactics in small and large groups, and firing and cleaning their weapon. There was also classroom instruction: military courtesy and discipline, articles of war, organization of the Army, guard duty, first aid, personal hygiene and field sanitation, uniforms, protecting military secrets and information on the enemy.

But Mount Currahee would not prove to be the biggest challenge Easy Company would face at Toccoa. Easy Company was different from the other units at Toccoa. That was because Easy's commander was Captain Herbert M. Sobel. By all accounts, Sobel was widely disliked by the men under his command. Sobel would find the smallest reasons to create punishments, causing them to lose privileges, like weekend leave from the camp, or forcing them to do more physical training (PT). The men relied on each other to endure and get past the constant inspections for the minutest amount of dirt on their gear or uniforms. Sobel would constantly conduct surprise inspections of the barracks, looking for more reasons to punish the men.

Sobel had the men march on Friday nights instead of having the night off to relax, like the other companies. The marches started out at five miles and added five miles each week. The longest march was 50 miles with no food, no water, no talking and no stopping. And Captain Sobel was there to check canteens at the end, to make sure no one had a sip of water.

While Sobel's training regime was a burden for Easy Company, one thing is for sure -- it added to the bond of brotherhood. The men gained confidence in their ability to endure and succeed together against tough demands. Additionally, the men realized it made them very physically fit as Easy held the fitness record in the 506th. However, the Army officials in Washington D. C. did not believe the results could be so impressive and sent an officer down to re-test Easy Company...they scored even higher!

Easy Company's second-in-command was Executive Officer (XO) Lieutenant Richard "Dick" Winters. Lt. Winters was a leader the men trusted and relied upon during the days of hard training and especially, during all the days of harsh punishments from Sobel.

Easy Company needed Lt. Winters, and he would prove to never let them down.

MARCH TO ATLANTA

Colonel Sink read an article in *Reader's Digest* magazine about a unit from the Japanese army that broke the world record for marching. Sink's strong beliefs in his training regime and in his men inspired him to march the 2nd battalion of the 506th from Camp Toccoa to Atlanta from December 1-3, 1942. The march took 75 hours and 15 minutes, with over 33 hours of strenuous marching. Just eight miles outside Toccoa, the marchers encountered horrendous weather conditions, including thick fog, heavy rain, mud up to their knees and freezing temperatures at night, all the while, marching 38-40 miles a day. Even more challenging, they carried their full battle equipment including rifles, mortars, tents and radio equipment. The men traded out the 36-pound machine gun and the 42-pound 60mm mortar so no one man would have to suffer the weight alone.

The icy roads resulted in a few sprained ankles. Soldiers would help carry the gear of their injured buddies. Some of the guys were carrying three rifles, so that more muscles could be used to help the injured.

By the time the men finished the first day, darkness had overtaken the terrain. Everyone struggled to stay warm. Army regulations required a paratrooper to change his socks every night. The men who made the mistake of taking off their boots to sleep found the leather frozen stiff the next morning, and it took several hours of marching to loosen their boots again. Thus, they learned to leave their boots on, all the way to Atlanta – even while sleeping. Sometimes, rules had to be broken. Even under the miserable weather conditions, Lt. Winters circulated among the men encouraging them to, "Hang tough."

On the second day, Private Don Malarkey's shin splints were causing him so much pain that he was crawling on his hands and knees to get to chow (army slang for food). His buddy Warren "Skip" Muck said, "No friend of mine crawls anywhere," and brought Don his food. Malarkey spent three days in bed after reaching Atlanta because his legs were so swollen.

The men of the battalion were not the only ones on the trek. "Draftee" was a brown and white puppy that followed the march for several miles. The dog had a limp, so the men picked up the pup and put it into Private First Class DeWitt Lowrey's backpack. Once Easy Company reached Ft. Benning, the next stop after marching to Atlanta, "Draftee" was given to the nurses on base.

Such early adversity did not deter the men of Easy Company, as they could be heard singing and laughing and issuing verbal challenges to Hitler, Germany's dictator. These early trials and the harsh conditions only served to help strengthen the bond among the men of Easy Company that would eventually evolve into a brotherhood.

As the 506th entered Atlanta, high school bands played and people lined the streets cheering. The *Atlanta Constitution* newspaper did a few interviews with the men and took photographs. No doubt, those proud and invigorated paratroopers forgot a little bit of the pain of sore feet, legs and backs as they marched into Atlanta, and into the record books, with chests stuck out and heads held high! Only twelve out of the 556 enlisted men failed to finish the march. All of the thirty officers finished.

Colonel Sink was proud.

JUMP SCHOOL

After the march into Atlanta, Easy Company boarded trains to Ft. Benning, GA, for parachute training. Instantly, they were struck by the four immense 250-foot towers overlooking the camp, three of which are still in use today. Jump school was divided into four stages and took 26 days of lectures, written tests and hands-on training:

A Stage: The first week was constant physical training for eight hours a day, six days a week. Strength and endurance were essential characteristics for paratroopers. In addition to the usual rope climbing, push-ups, runs during the day and night, some paratrooper-specific training was added: judo training taught hand-to-hand combat, while tumbling exercises helped with breaking the fall during a jump. This week was a test of not only physical abilities, but also, mental toughness. Such a strenuous training schedule washed out many guys of the paratroops. Easy and the rest of the 506th arrived at Ft. Benning in better shape than the cadre (instructors). The surprised cadre was forced to admit that the 506th could skip this stage.

B Stage: This week was dedicated to teaching the men, while on the ground, how to parachute. They learned the parts of the parachute, proper body position from the moment they exited the plane to the moment they landed and performed the Parachute Landing Fall (PLF). Landing properly in order to minimize injury was paramount to a successful mission. This week also introduced the 34-foot tower. Strapped into webbing gear that went around the crotch and torso, soldiers climbed the stairs of the tower and were then attached to a harness and pulley that sloped down from the tower to a sand pit; similar to a modern zip-line. The men had to stand in the mock door with the proper form and jumped out on command. The men fell several feet, simulating the free fall from the aircraft prior to the parachute opening. The pulley snapped and they traveled down the "zip line" to simulate the speed of a landing, performing a proper PLF at the end. The "zip line" had different angles, so the students experienced the reality of varying wind conditions that affect landing. The men were graded on all aspects of the "jump" and repeated the process.

PLF: Initially paratrooper trainees were taught to do a somersault upon landing. But new tactics learned by the British led to the development of the PLF. Soldiers kept their feet and knees together and slightly bent the knees. Starting at the balls of their feet on up, the muscles from the calf, thigh, and side of the upper body allowed the absorption of the landing's impact by rolling on their sides.

C Stage: Soldiers continued using the 34-foot towers, the suspended harness trainer and began using the 250-foot towers. They also continued to the use the mock-door trainer to simulate mass exits of the aircraft. The soldiers practiced and practiced and practiced until they could exit two men every second. The quicker they could exit the plane, the closer they would land together on the ground and the faster they could join together and survive to complete the mission.

Additionally, soldiers also learned the jump phases: aircraft exit, opening shock and parachute deployment and steering the parachute to landing. Another critical skill learned was dealing with a parachute malfunction and the possible deployment of the reserve parachute. They also became schooled in oscillation (swinging back and forth) and how to recover from being dragged. Large fans were used to blow the parachuted soldier across the ground to familiarize him with the way the wind could catch the parachute after landing. The soldier would roll his body until he could get to his feet, and then run toward the parachute, which allowed the parachute to deflate.

The men had plenty of incentive to pay close attention to learning all the details of parachute packing. They would jump with the parachute they themselves packed!

JUMP WEEK

DStage or Jump Week: Finally putting into practice all the skills learned while on the ground, soldiers were required to complete five jumps, with one jump at night and two jumps with full combat gear. After painstakingly following all the steps of packing their own parachute, they loaded in the planes in "sticks" of 18-20 men. The nervous tension began to build.

The Jumpmaster is either the instructor or in combat, the lead jumper in the "stick." Everyone would follow his commands. Over the noise of the aircraft, the jumpmaster would call out how many minutes until reaching the drop zone (DZ), and the men would yell back the time they heard. This repetition by the jumpers was vital to make certain every man in the "stick" heard the commands and were coordinated in the preparation for the jump. The jumpmaster would yell, "Get ready!" and the men readied their gear and buckled their helmets' chinstraps.

The jumpmaster would yell, "Stand up!" which the men yelled back as they stood, and the command, "Hook up!" was quickly yelled next. In his hand, each soldier tightly held a metal hook that he attached to a cable that ran overhead, the length of the plane's interior. The hook attached to a cord which led to the parachute on their backs. Once the men jumped, the fall caused the cord to automatically pull the parachute from the pack so it could deploy.

Once the men were hooked in, the jumpmaster yelled, "Sound off for equipment check!" The men again quickly but carefully scrutinized their gear and their buddy's gear in front of them to make sure all the straps were buckled, hardware was snapped tightly and no items were loose or out of place. Verifying the equipment check was paramount to the safety of the men and the success of the jump. The men reported from the back to the front of the plane, "Twenty ok!," "Nineteen ok!," etc.

The jumpmaster yelled, "One minute!" and the men repeated.

"Stand in the door!" was the command to the first jumper and the men behind shuffled up closer toward the door. "GO!" and the jumpmaster's slap on the shoulder sent the "stick" into the blue skies.

The soldiers counted, "one-thousand-one, one-thousand-two, one-thousand-three" and then looked up to make sure the parachute had fully deployed. If the main parachute failed to deploy after three seconds, the soldier wasted no more time and deployed the reserve parachute on his chest, for there had been a malfunction in his main parachute.

Training jumps were made between 600 and 1,500 feet, depending on the time of day, wind speed and amount of gear being worn. The qualification jumps were usually at 1,000 feet. The jumpers were able to enjoy the view as they descended and were sometimes close enough to have a conversation.

There were no second chances for anyone who froze on a jump. Each second that passed between jumpers caused a greater distance between each paratrooper once they landed, thus, reducing the ability for the entire stick to come together quickly as a group and begin the mission. While it may seem harsh, freezing on the jump was an instant disqualification from jump training and the soldier was immediately removed from the entire base and transferred to a regular Army unit. During war, lives could be lost on a scattered jump. There could be no hesitation. Little has changed since WWII regarding the training, discipline and attention to detail for those who strive to graduate from jump school.

The C-47 *Skytrain* (as the Americans called it) or *Dakota* (as the British called it) transport airplane was used to carry the paratroopers. Over 10,000 were built during WWII. In addition to transporting troops, it could air-drop supplies or tow a glider behind it.

The Army afforded most of the men their first time to fly in an airplane. For a few, it was their first time to ever see an airplane. These men made many practice jumps, both in America and in Europe, and while they had taken off numerous times in the planes, even after leaving the Army and returning home, almost every one of them had yet to actually land in an airplane...they had always parachuted out!

JUMP BOOTS AND JUMP WINGS

Back in the 1940s, and still true today, those men who successfully completed jump school participated in an elaborate graduation ceremony. Many of the men said it was one of the proudest moments of their lives. The new paratroopers were presented with their silver "Army Parachutist Badge" or Jump Wings, which were pinned to the left chest. Maybe more importantly, the men were allowed to wear their jump boots off the training base. Wearing those jump boots and tucking their pant legs into them (known as 'blousing') instantly differentiated the paratrooper from ALL other troops in any branch of service. It was a source of pride that paratroopers took very seriously. Putting it mildly, these men had worked extremely hard to earn the right to wear jump boots and blouse their pants!

Paratroopers called all the other soldiers, "legs" which was a slang term for non-paratroopers whose pants were "straight legged." If paratroopers saw "legs" blousing their pants, it was guaranteed to create some fighting words and very possibly, some fighting fists.

When weekend passes were given, inspections by the Sergeant were often required before leaving base. Everything had to be perfect on the paratrooper's uniform, especially when they were in public. The pants and shirts had to have razor sharp creases, and those jump boots had to shine!

The jump boots were sometimes called paratrooper boots or "Corcorans" as they were made by the Corcoran and Matterhorn Company. Paratroopers would 'ladder lace' their boots, a technique to help with ankle support for parachute landings. Corcoran continues to make their paratrooper boots today.

For each combat parachute jump, a bronze star was attached to the jump wings. Most of the men in Easy Company earned one or two bronze star attachments, for the Normandy and Holland jumps. Captain Lewis Nixon was one of four members of Easy Company (and one of the few in the entire 101st Airborne) to complete three combat jumps and earn his third bronze star for his jump wings. Nixon was temporarily attached to the 17th Airborne Division during *Operation Varsity*, the airborne crossing of the Rhine River into Germany while Easy Company was recuperating in Mourmelon, France.

The other three Easy members to earn a third attachment on their jump wings were Pathfinders Corporal Richard Wright, Corporal Carl Fenstermaker and Private Lavon Reese. Pathfinders were volunteers inside the already volunteer paratrooper units. They had the specific mission of parachuting about one hour before everyone else, in groups of just 8-10 men, in order to assist the large oncoming force land more accurately on the drop zone. Pathfinders used specialized equipment, such as radio transmitters, to help guide the lead planes to the drop zone.

PATCHES AND BADGES

THE PARA-DICE PATCH

This design consists of an eagle diving with a parachute canopy in the background. The "pair of dice" shows a "5" and "6" which are connected by a large, black "0" -- spelling out 506th. These designs together, represented the 506th as a parachute unit, attacking from the sky. Once the 506th was attached to the 101st Airborne, the patch became an unauthorized insignia. As a matter of pride, however, the men again ignored Army regulations and proudly donned the patch on the front of their jump uniforms or leather jackets.

THE DISTINCTIVE UNIT INSIGNIA

Still worn today, the blue field on this metal insignia represents the Infantry, the 506th Parachute Infantry Regiment's branch of service. The thunderbolt represents, then and now, the regiment's specific threat and ability to attack from the sky, striking with speed, power and surprise. Six parachutes characterize the 506th as the sixth parachute regiment activated in the U. S. Army. The green silhouette across the bottom symbolizes Currahee Mountain, the site of the regiment's activation in Toccoa, Georgia. The mountain also symbolizes the regiment's strength, independence and ability to "stand alone" against the enemy, a trait for which the proud paratroopers are well-known.

THE 101st AIRBORNE SHOULDER PATCH

The 101st Airborne patch is one of the most recognizable shoulder patches in the U. S. Army, still today. It has given the division the nickname, the "Screaming Eagles."

The eagle is a tribute to "Old Abe," a real-life Bald Eagle born in 1861 that was named after President Abraham Lincoln. Old Abe was the mascot of the 8th Wisconsin Volunteer Infantry Regiment that fought against the Confederate Army during the Civil War. And Old Abe was present at all their battles, carried by a sergeant on a special perch.

In 1921, the 101st Infantry Division was created as a reserve unit in WWI. Even though the unit never saw combat, the patch was again used as their identifier. When the 101st Airborne was reactivated as a paratrooper division in 1942, the "Old Abe" patch with its long history was chosen to represent them, yet again.

AIRBORNE

Currahee

STATUE OF LIBERTY

From May to July, 1943, the men traveled by train to join other units in the 101st for large-scale combat training exercises at Camp MacKall, North Carolina and then in Kentucky, Tennessee and Indiana. The exercises were the Army's largest training for paratroopers. For realism, the men slept in tents and ate field rations. They wondered if they would be sent to fight the Germans in Europe or the Japanese in the Pacific.

In August of 1943, they had their answer. The men of Easy Company joined the rest of the 101st Airborne in Camp Shanks, New York, not far from New York City. The next stop was England to confront the Germans. All members of the 101st Airborne had to remove their "Screaming Eagle" patch and they could not wear their jump boots, in an effort to prevent any observing German spies from knowing an elite airborne force was headed to Europe for the invasion.

Capt. Sobel wrote a letter to the mothers of the men before they left:

Dear Madam: Soon your son will drop from the sky to engage and defeat the enemy. He will have the best of weapons, and equipment, and has had months of hard, strenuous training to prepare him for success on the battlefield. Your frequent letters of love and encouragement will arm him with a fighting heart. With that, he cannot fail, but will win glory for himself, make you proud of him, and his country ever grateful for his service in its hour of need.

Herbert M. Sobel, Capt., Commanding.

The men boarded the long, steep gangplank. The *S. S. Samaria* was meant to hold 1,000 people; this voyage it would carry 5,000. The men gathered at the ship's railing and waved at people in boats in the harbor. Shortly after setting sail, Bill Guarnere saluted the Statue of Liberty as they passed. The *Samaria*, part of a large convoy of over 100 ships, steered in a zig-zag pattern to further confuse any possible German submarines patrolling the Atlantic Ocean looking for targets.

Two men were assigned to each bunk bed, which were stacked four high, with barely enough room to turn over. Each man would alternate between sleeping in the bunk bed and sleeping on the open deck outside under the stars. Many of the men learned to enjoy the open deck, compared to the cramped quarters below.

The daily routine on the ship was far from exciting and mealtime didn't help. The food was prepared by British cooks and included boiled fish, tomatoes and thin slices of bread. Needless to say, the meals, on top of the ocean waves, did not sit well with the Americans' stomachs and the men often sought out candy bars and cookies to survive.

The showers consisted of cold saltwater and drinking water was only available a few hours per day. Many of the men passed on the cold showers and they began to stink, especially in the close confines below the deck. Between lifeboat drills and weapons inspections, the men spent their time reading, talking about home, gambling or playing cards.

For almost every man, it was their first trip outside America. No doubt, thoughts of home and loved ones filled the minds of the men as they watched America fade into the horizon. Months and months of structure during training now turned into days and days of uncertainty, floating on the open ocean. It took twelve days to reach England.

Easy Company moved closer to war.

Sobel and Winters...Aldbourne to Upottery

Easy Company settled in the small, quiet village of Aldbourne, in southern England. But life under Sobel's rule was far from quiet as he constantly shouted at the men and never smiled or joked around. The smallest infraction could result in latrine (toilet) duty for the guilty party. Lt. Winters was still second in command and just about the exact opposite of Sobel. While both were in excellent physical shape, Winters was respectful and calm. Maybe more importantly, he was fair with the men regarding Army rules. Even though they admired Sobel's desire for Easy Company to be the best in the 101st Airborne, the men felt that Winters, unlike Sobel, genuinely cared about their welfare. They watched the growing animosity between Sobel and Winters; the gulf between the different leadership philosophies widened.

However, daily training continued and intensified with hand-to-hand fighting, digging foxholes, first aid, hand signals and chemical warfare knowledge. Jump training was done more often with full combat gear, and the men practiced steering away from trees and water by using the risers (cords that connected to the parachute). Private Rudolph Dittrich was lost during training when his parachute failed to open, reminding each paratrooper that their role was filled with extra danger.

As the days turned into weeks, the men grew ever more distrustful of Sobel's ability to lead during the training exercises. Training required longer days and nights in the field, hiking through the woods to practice staying together and staying quiet. But Sobel was loud when walking in the woods, and he would constantly get the men lost by poor map reading, even leading the men into ambushes on practice attacks against other units. Walking into an ambush in war would cost the men their lives! If Sobel was ineffective with the most basic of techniques required of an infantryman, like map reading and assault tactics, how could he lead the men during battle? It was a constant question the men asked each other. The battle between Sobel and Winters soon exploded and Easy Company would be forever changed.

In October, 1943, Sobel gave Winters an order to inspect the latrines at 10:00 a.m. Unbeknownst to Winters, Sobel had changed the time to 9:45 a.m. When Winters was "late" for the inspection, Sobel took away Winters' weekend pass as punishment; a typical move for Sobel. But Winters finally stood his ground, writing, "I request trial by Courts Martial for failure to inspect the latrines at 0945 (9:45 a.m.) this date." His bold demand initiated a formal investigation, which meant Winters was transferred to supervise the kitchen during the process; a demoralizing role for Winters, who just wanted to be with his soldiers.

The NCOs (Non-Commissioned Officers, who are Sergeants) had finally had enough after Sobel attempted to discipline Winters over something so minor as a latrine inspection. They wrote letters of resignation to Colonel Sink, an action that during a time of war, could have led to them being shot for treason. But the action reflected just how strongly the NCOs felt about Sobel's negative leadership skills as they prepared for war.

Colonel Sink was furious at the NCOs! Sink demoted some of them in rank; others he transferred to different companies in the 506th. In the end, Colonel Sink knew he could not keep Sobel in charge of Easy Company. He transferred the embattled commander to the Chilton Foliet training camp in England to help teach civilians, such as chaplains and doctors, to be jump-certified in order to parachute with the soldiers into battle.

Lieutenant Thomas Meehan was transferred from Baker Company to lead Easy Company. Winters was brought back to Easy Company and became 1st Platoon's leader. Easy Company was finally calm and now in safe leadership hands. It was a significant move because on May 29, 1944, the men loaded into trucks and left Aldbourne and headed further south to Upottery Airfield, where rows of C-47s waited for their cargo of paratroopers. The men left all non-essential luggage behind.

War was looming.

WEAPONS

The **M-1 Garand** was the main infantry rifle used by all branches of the armed services in WWII. Approximately 5,400,000 were made during the war and it was in use for almost 30 years, well into the 1960s. The famous General George S. Patton called it "the greatest battle implement ever devised." Fed from the top by an eight-round clip and weighing almost 10 pounds, it had an effective range of 500 yards.

Over 1,500,000 of the **Thompson sub-machine guns,** nicknamed the "Tommy Gun," were produced for the military during WWII. The Thompson, having a 20-round magazine, was a prized possession by those lucky enough to get one. Often, they were given to NCOs, but those leading patrols preferred to have one because of its rapid rate of fire and its effectiveness in ranges from 50-75 yards, although it had a top range of about 150 yards.

Attached to the weapons platoon, the **M-2 60 millimeter mortar** required a squad of 3-4 men to successfully operate it. Approximately 60,000 were made during WWII. It was fired by dropping the mortar round into the top of the tube. After a couple of seconds, the round fired automatically. This heavy weapon was essential for paratroopers, who lacked armored support. The mortar was manned by a squad leader, a gunner and a loader and sometimes, ammunition carriers were attached to the squad as well. The mortar was broken down into three parts; the base plate, the firing tube and the tripod, all of which weighed a total of 42 pounds. Each mortar round weighed three pounds and had a range of 200 to 2,000 yards, depending on the angle of the firing tube. A trained crew could fire 18 - 20 rounds per minute. Since the mortar was fired in an upward arc, it was an effective weapon when targets were hidden by terrain, like forests or buildings or on the other side of levees (as was the case in The Netherlands).

D-DAY – OVERVIEW

The invasion of mainland Europe during WWII was the largest military operation of all time and it was close to a year in the planning stages. American servicemen numbering in the neighborhood of 1,400,000 had arrived in Britain, and by the time the offensive attack was ready to begin, another 600,000 troops from Britain, Canada, Australia, Belgium, France, The Netherlands, Poland, New Zealand, Norway, Greece and Czechoslovakia had joined the fray.

Operation Overlord was the code name for the Battle of Normandy in France; the Allies' operation that launched the invasion of German-occupied Europe on June 6, 1944 (D-Day). General Dwight Eisenhower (later President of the United States) commanded all the nations' forces.

All information regarding the invasion was marked as "BIGOT" which was a classification higher than even "Top Secret." "BIGOT" stood for **B**ritish **I**nvasion of **G**erman **O**ccupied **T**erritory. British Prime Minister Winston Churchill created the acronym before America entered the war, and it remained a security clearance after Eisenhower was in command. Every person with knowledge of the D-Day operation was added to the "BIGOT list." Those on the list were not allowed to travel outside the United Kingdom, in case they were captured and made to reveal the secrets. Of course, Churchill himself was the only exception to the travel ban.

The Allies made over 3,200 photo-reconnaissance flights from April 1944 until the start of the invasion in June, taking photos of the coastline at extremely low altitude to show the troops the terrain, obstacles on the beach, and defensive structures such as bunkers and gun emplacements. In an effort to further confuse the Germans and to avoid alerting them as to the exact location of the invasion, the planes had to fly over the entire European coastline.

While the Germans knew an invasion was imminent, they could not determine the precise site. Thus, Adolf Hitler placed German Field Marshal Erwin Rommel in charge of creating fortifications all along the coastline in anticipation of an attack, building an "Atlantic Wall." This "wall" was 2,400 miles long and made of concrete bunkers, barbed wire, machine guns. Rommel also created steel obstacles to prevent ships from landing on the beach and prohibiting tanks from being able to traverse the terrain. Additionally, Rommel positioned over 5,000,000 landmines along the front with the sole intent of repelling any assault and pushing enemy forces back into the Atlantic Ocean.

The Allies used the famous General George Patton to help convince the Germans that the invasion would come at Pas de Calais, France; a logical location as it was the shortest distance between England and France. Using inflatable tanks and airplanes that were set up so they would be seen by German airplanes performing reconnaissance, a group of 1,100 specialists developed an elaborate deception plan. Further adding to their ruse, they initiated fake radio transmissions to simulate movements of large groups of troops in the area. The designed trickery had the desired outcome because 150,000 German troops, plus tanks, stayed in the Pas de Calais area for weeks after the actual invasion, keeping them out of the fight in Normandy.

As the time for the attack drew near, Eisenhower and his Allied commanders selected a 50-mile stretch of the coast in Normandy as the site for the invasion. The Americans were assigned to land at sectors code named *Utah* and *Omaha*, the British at *Sword* and *Gold* and the Canadians at *Juno*.

You are about to embark upon the Great Crusade, toward which we have striven these many months. The eyes of the world are upon you. The hopes and prayers of liberty-loving people everywhere march with you. In company with our brave Allies and brothers-in-arms on other fronts, you will bring about the destruction of the German war machine, the elimination of Nazi tyranny over the oppressed peoples of Europe, and security for ourselves in a free world.

—Eisenhower, Letter to Allied Forces

Because a full moon was required to assist the paratroopers in their ability to see the drop zones, only a limited number of nights each month were available. Additionally, in order to avoid the numerous German obstacles and mines placed along the coast, the successful assault also needed a high ocean tide, which further limited the opportunities on the calendar. The original date for the invasion was June 5th, but bad weather pushed it to the 6th.

Prior to the invasion, 1,000 bombers a day were performing air strikes on German airfields, bridges, railroads and military installations in France. Because of this strategy, the Luftwaffe, the German air force, was basically non-existent on D-Day; even more impressive was the fact that no Allied planes were shot down in air-to-air combat.

On D-Day, 24,000 paratroopers preceded the beach invasions with their jumps. The U.S. 82nd and 101st Airborne Divisions were joined by the British 6th Airborne Division. Due to heavy German air artillery fire, only 15% of the paratroopers landed at the planned locations. Though scattered, the paratroopers gathered together from different units to form fighting teams and moved toward their correct locations and objectives.

The scattered landings had the secondary effect of further confusing the Germans as to the exact location of the drops and also, just how many paratroopers were landing. Another diversionary effort unfolded as hundreds of sand-filed dummies, named "Ruperts" were dropped by parachute to distract the Germans from the real drop zones. These dummies closely resembled actual paratroopers, and because some were made to explode when they hit the ground, additional chaos resulted on the part of the Germans.

The naval bombardment from five huge battleships, twenty cruisers, sixty-five destroyers and two British monitor warships began at 5:45 a.m. and continued until 6:25 a.m. Arriving from the sea shortly thereafter were over 4,000 landing craft that would deliver 132,000 men.

However, all this manpower and firepower was not enough to stop the substantial loss of lives at *Omaha*, the most heavily defended sector. The U. S. 1st Infantry Division, supplemented by troops from the U.S. 29th Division, faced an entire German division rather than just the expected single regiment. Confronting overwhelming firepower from the cliffs above resulted in more U.S. casualties at this site than at all the other beach landings combined.

Fate, in addition to the intelligent strategy, played an enormous role in the outcome of the battle. The Allies benefited from the fact that the Germans were left without some key leadership decision makers. Believing the seas would be too rough for the Allies to land, Field Marshal Rommel was on leave back home in Germany for his wife's birthday. Additionally, only Hitler could authorize the movement of the German tanks and fearing his wrath, no one wanted to wake him from his sleep to inform him of the invasion. Because Hitler slept until around noon that day, those tanks were delayed in reaching the battlefield.

While D-Day was a success in that it established a beach-head for getting troops, equipment and supplies onto the mainland, the cost of life was high. Over 9,000 Allied soldiers were wounded or killed that day alone.

D-Day – Easy Company

Before the mission, the cooks prepared a wonderful meal for Easy Company: steak and potatoes, peas, bread with butter, and for dessert – ice cream! It was the best meal the Army had ever given them.

The men blackened their faces with shoe polish. Paratroopers had big, extra pockets on their pants and jackets to carry the required gear since there were no supplies available when they landed behind enemy lines. In their pants pockets, they had K-rations, a package of food which was supposed to last three days. In backpacks, called musette bags, they carried a poncho, blanket, toiletries and mess kit (plate, spoon, cup). The belt around their waist held ten clips of M-1 rifle ammunition (80 rounds total), a small shovel (entrenching tool), canteen, bayonet and gas mask (which the men threw away after landing). Most of the men wore suspenders that held grenades and a pistol. Paratroopers put their fixed-blade knife on the side of their boot and a small switchblade knife in a zippered pocket next to the jacket collar. This knife was easily accessible should they land in a tree and have to cut the risers to get down. They would also carry 33 feet of rope in case they needed to get down after landing in a tree.

Added to all this gear was a steel helmet, a main parachute on their back, a reserve parachute on their chest, and a yellow life jacket. The machine gunners and mortar men had their weapons too, and their ammunition was spread around for others to help carry. Medics and radio men had their specific equipment as well. With all that gear, it was difficult to even walk. Sometimes it took two to four men to help one man climb aboard the C-47.

The paratroopers were given a small children's toy called a "cricket." Pressing it made a "click-clack" sound. Landing in the dark made identifying friends and foes very difficult. A paratrooper would click once and the other person would click twice. Thus, both knew they were friends. Without a cricket, the men used passwords on D-Day. The challenger would say, "Flash" and the correct response was, "Thunder." The passwords were then changed every day.

Shortly after midnight, the groups of C-47s took off. The planes joined together in formations shaped like a "V" and three sets of "Vs" joined again to make a larger V-formation. Dim red lights inside the plane lit the men's faces. The loud engines made talking impossible. A few of the men slept. Some prayed. Everyone was lost in thoughts of what his first experiences in combat would bring. The Germans waited behind their "Atlantic Wall."

Just prior to boarding the C-47s, Bill Guarnere, the soldier who had saluted the Statue of Liberty, accidentally found out that his brother had been killed in the fighting in Italy. He wanted revenge. And in the Normandy fighting, he would earn his nickname, "Wild Bill" for exacting some of his revenge upon the enemy.

As the planes approached the coast, the anti-aircraft fire began reaching toward the sky. The men could hear pieces of shrapnel "tinging" against the metal of the plane. In some places, they could see the large bullet holes slice all the way through the floor to the roof of the plane. Coming from the ground, every third or fourth bullet were tracers of green, red and blue, which aided the Germans in shooting in the dark.

The pilots steered the planes left and right, up and down, trying to avoid being hit, tossing the paratroopers everywhere. The feeling of helplessness was overwhelming and thousands of impatient paratroopers wanted out of those planes. When the green lights came on inside, the men wasted no time jumping! Instinctively, many of the pilots increased the planes' speed in an attempt to avoid being shot down. Those troopers jumped with the plane going too fast, which ripped their equipment and weapons off their bodies; they landed surrounded by the enemy, in the dark, alone, and with only a knife strapped on their boot. Still others saw the tracers burning holes through their parachute as they floated to the ground, another very helpless feeling. So much evasive maneuvering by the pilots meant almost everyone landed in the wrong place.

General Taylor, commander of the 101st Airborne, promised only three days and three nights of fighting...it was not meant to be.

BRÉCOURT MANOR

Easy Company was supposed to land around the village of Marie-du-Mont, but most of the paratroopers were scattered, leaving them with the task of walking and fighting their way to reconnect with the unit.

Lt. Winters located a group of 2nd Battalion soldiers in the hamlet of Le Grand Chemin. Those daylight hours of June 6, 1944, found Winters to be the highest ranking officer of Easy Company. However, most of his men were nowhere to be found. Unknown at the time, Stick #66, with Easy's Commanding Officer, Lt. Thomas Meehan, had been shot down; with no survivors.

Winters was ordered to take out a German artillery battery firing on U.S. troops coming ashore on *Utah* Beach, about three miles away. The battery, located at Brécourt Manor farm, had escaped detection from the pre-invasion intelligence gathering. With no other information available, Winters, always leading from the front, went out on his own to perform reconnaissance. He found four German 105mm cannons, connected by a series of trenches. The cannons were defended by approximately 60 German soldiers. The odds were not in Winters' favor and he knew surprise was going to be his biggest ally in the attack.

Winters split his twelve men in two groups and ordered two machine guns set up to divide the Germans' attention. Winters began the attack with, "Follow me!" Winters and his men moved forward, crouched over in the trenches to avoid detection. Armed with grenades and rifles, they quickly confronted the Germans at the first cannon. Each of the four cannons had to be destroyed one at a time, all the while defending against and eliminating the German troops, who also had their own machine guns set up in the field. One by one, the Americans placed a block of TNT down the enemy barrel and used grenades to set off the TNT, destroying the cannons.

Later, six men from Dog, Fox and Headquarters (HQ) companies came up as reinforcements and the last cannon was eliminated. Winters found a German map that marked all the artillery and machine gun positions in the Normandy area. This invaluable information was given to Winters' friend, and intelligence officer, Lt. Lewis Nixon.

For his superior leadership, Colonel Sink recommended Winters for the Medal of Honor, but it was downgraded to the next highest award, the Distinguished Service Cross. The following medals were also given for the action:

<u>Silver Star</u>
2nd Lt. Lynn "Buck" Compton, Sgt. William "Will Bill" Guarnere, PFC Gerald Lorraine

<u>Bronze Star</u>
Sgt. Carwood Lipton, Pvt. Robert "Popeye" Wynn (Purple Heart), Pvt. Cleveland Petty, Pvt. Walter Hendrix, Pvt. Don Malarkey, Pvt. Myron Ranney, Pvt. Joseph Liebgott, Pvt. John Plesha, Cpl. Joe Toye, PFC John D. Hall (Killed in Action (KIA), Purple Heart), Sgt. Julius "Rusty" Houch (KIA, Purple Heart)

Winters spoke on the events: *Years later, I heard from someone who had come up from the beach on that causeway. This guy, a medic, had been following behind some tanks. As they come up from the beach, one of the tanks became disabled. When the driver got out, he stepped on a mine. The medics went into the field and patched this guy up. Later, after the book came out (in 1992), the medic wrote me a letter and pointed out that he always wondered why the fire on Utah Beach had stopped. "Thanks very much." He said. "I couldn't have made it without those guns being knocked out." That medic later became a U. S. Attorney General. So, we did a little good out there for the troops coming in on D-Day, which makes you feel pretty good.* (<u>American History Magazine</u>, August 2004, by Chris Anderson).

CARENTAN

On June 12th, Easy Company and the 506th came to Carentan. The town was occupied by the Germans, but the Americans desperately needed to take it over in order to unite the forces from *Omaha* and *Utah* Beaches.

Lt. Winters gave the word for Easy to kick off the attack at dawn. Easy Company entered the town down a slightly sloping street that led to a T-intersection. The soldiers stormed down the street just as a German machine-gun nest opened fire, along with rifle fire from the building dead ahead. Easy took cover in the ditches, lying there like sitting ducks. Knowing that his men had to get moving or risk sure death, Winters stood in the middle of the street, frantically screaming and literally kicking and grabbing the men to get them moving forward. Amazingly, Winters was not hit by the flying bullets that pelted the ground all around him. His stunned men looked on in disbelief. Normally calm even under pressure, this was a side of Winters they had never seen. The men were motivated to continue forward on the attack.

Thanks to the quick action of Lt. Harry Welsh who was able to single-handedly take out the machine gun with a grenade, Easy successfully secured the intersection. Winters proved his leadership skills once again by being a source of inspiration for his troops.

Easy Company then proceeded from building to building, clearing out the Germans. However, this was just the beginning as Easy realized they were up against their German paratrooper counterparts, the *Fallschirmjäger*. The initial attack left ten injured, including a severely wounded Ed Tipper.

Winters found an injured soldier, Private Albert Blithe, at the aid station. When asked where he was injured, Blithe responded to his commander's query by stating that he could not see. Blithe was suffering from a condition known as "hysterical blindness," a condition that can be brought on by the stress of heavy battle. Winters offered Blithe some reassuring words. A while later, Blithe stood up and delightedly exclaimed he could see again. Among Winters' skills were his words of encouragement, which helped this young soldier recover from the shock of combat and to rejoin his buddies. Combat can do some strange things to the mind and the body.

Well into the next day, Easy Company and the rest of the 506th doggedly pursued the Germans on the outskirts of Carentan. During the final battle for the town, a German tank charged toward Easy's lines. Lt. Welsh and Private John McGrath ran heroically into the open field and straight into the path of the oncoming tank. They fired a bazooka round into the tank's unarmored belly, totally disabling it. With the arrival of the U.S. 2nd Armored Division and their tanks, the Americans triumphantly pushed the Germans out of Carentan.

Carentan would be the last battle for the 101st Airborne in Normandy. For Easy, it was one of the most intense battles they would endure during the war. The men were dirty, tired and had not had a shower in weeks. On July 1st, Winters was told he had been promoted to Captain, a rank he had been performing since June 6th, as Easy's *de facto* commander.

General Taylor had promised the men just three days of fighting. Three days had turned into thirty-five days of hard combat. The trip back to England would be on the water and Easy Company loaded up on a transport LST (Landing Ship Tank) and returned to Aldbourne. The entire 101st Airborne Division would be awarded the Distinguished Unit Citation for its actions in Normandy.

The campaign had cost Easy Company almost 50% of their men.

LAUNDRY

When the American GIs (slang for soldiers who were, "Government Issue") arrived in the United Kingdom in 1944, the British had been fighting against Germany since 1939. Part of Germany's plan in their battle against Britain was the use of submarines to sink the ships bringing supplies to the island, greatly decreasing necessary goods, especially food. Germany thought they could starve the British into submission. As a result, almost everything was already rationed: gasoline, bacon and ham, butter, sugar, meat, tea, jelly, cheese, eggs, milk, fruit, soap, paper and clothing. Even Christmas trees were nearly impossible to find due to the timber rationing. Everyone on both sides of the Atlantic Ocean found obtaining these articles, as well as many luxuries, most difficult. Almost every household item was needed for the war effort, and everyone sacrificed for the goal of winning the war. Rationing in England did not end with final battle. The war required so many goods that final rationing concluded eight years after the war ended, in 1953.

The GIs were paid significantly more than their British counterparts, so the Americans were able to indulge in such basic services like laundry while they were stationed in towns and villages around the English countryside. In turn, the local people could earn extra money.

Sometimes, events outside of battle make just as an indelible mark as those on the battlefield. Malarkey found himself in one of those moments. Now back in Aldbourne, Malarkey visited the woman who was cleaning some of Easy's laundry and collected his uniforms. Before Malarkey could leave, she asked if he would mind taking the laundry of some of the other guys to, "save them a trip." Glancing through the neatly stacked packages, Malarkey realized many of those men would not be in need of clean laundry. They had died fighting the Germans in Normandy. And though the moment struck Malarkey hard, he did not mention this personal cost of war to the innocent woman.

The Army taught them how to fight, how to survive, but not how to deal with losing their buddies. The noise and sights of warfare often prevent a soldier from processing the casualties of those around them at that moment; survival and the mission take precedence. Seeing those laundry bundles with the names of his fallen brothers carefully inscribed on them made the losses suddenly and unexpectedly real for Malarkey.

For the rest of his life, the encounter remained vivid memory.

MEDALS (U. S. ARMY)

The **Medal of Honor** (MoH) is the highest military decoration that may be awarded by the United States government, personally presented by the President of the United States in the name of the Congress. It is conferred only upon members of the United States Armed Forces who distinguish themselves through conspicuous gallantry and intrepidity at the risk of life above and beyond the call of duty. Each branch of the armed services has the blue ribbon and stars, but the medal itself is slightly different for each branch.

During WWII, 467 were awarded: 326 to the Army, 82 to the Marines, 58 to the Navy and 1 to the Coast Guard.

The **Distinguished Service Cross** (DSC) is the second-highest combat decoration and is awarded for extraordinary heroism.

The **Silver Star** is the third-highest combat decoration and is awarded for gallantry in action.

The **Bronze Star** is the fourth-highest combat decoration and is awarded for acts of heroism, acts of merit, or meritorious service in a combat zone.

The **Purple Heart** is awarded to military members who have been wounded or killed during combat.

The **Combat Medic Badge** is awarded to soldiers who perform medical duties while simultaneously engaged by the enemy. The two main symbols are the entwined serpents, representing the recipient's medical expertise and the horizontal stretcher, representing that expertise being rendered on the field of battle.

The **Combat Infantry Badge** (CIB) is awarded to infantry soldiers who actively fight in ground combat. The main focus of this badge is a 3-inch-wide rectangular bar with an infantry-blue field upon which is superimposed a Springfield Arsenal Musket, Model 1795. The rectangular bar is placed on top of an elliptic oak-leaf wreath, symbolizing steadfast character, strength, and loyalty.

* General Maxwell Taylor mandated that only one Medal of Honor was to be awarded in the 101st Airborne Division for all of the Normandy campaign. Lieutenant Colonel Robert G. Cole, commander of the 3rd Battalion, 502nd Parachute Infantry Regiment, was that sole recipient for leading a bayonet charge near Carentan. Col. Sink's recommendation for the Medal of Honor for Lt. Winters was therefore downgraded to the DSC.

OPERATION *MARKET-GARDEN*

Prior to the next operation, recuperation for Easy Company was the order of the day. Promotions also came along for those who had proven themselves leaders in combat. The main concerns were getting replacements for both soldiers and gear. Training, based on the lessons learned in Normandy, continued in order to keep the "veterans" sharp and to get the new replacements quickly up to speed. Men who were injured and in hospitals were eager to get back to their brothers in Easy so the Army would not reassign them to other units.

Operation *Market-Garden (Market:* Airborne troops*; Garden:* ground troops*)* was the plan to free The Netherlands. If successful, the men felt the war would be over by Christmas. As planned, but a surprise to the men, the jump would happen in the daylight instead of at night as they had done in Normandy. The strategy was to hold a 16-mile long narrow corridor of roads and bridges from Eindhoven to Arnhem. It was a risky and complicated plan because of the woody and marshy terrain, which limited the Allies' targets and allowed the Germans ample opportunities to flank from either side.

On September 17, 1944, over 1,400 C-47 *Dakota* transport planes carried the paratroopers while 450 gliders were towed from behind. In total, the force included 20,000 paratroopers and almost 15,000 glider troops. American glider troops were aboard the *Waco*, which was made of mostly plywood with some aluminum to strengthen the frame. Without an engine of its own, The *Waco* could carry 13 troops and would glide to the ground once released from the cable attached to the C-47.

The jumpers encountered much less German anti-aircraft artillery than in Normandy, and they landed in open, plowed fields. Due to the concentration of jumpers, who landed in very close proximity to one another on the DZ (drop zone), falling men and equipment proved to be more dangerous than the enemy on this particular jump. On the positive side, almost 90% of the troopers landed near their designated area – a far cry from the experiences in Normandy.

Once on the ground and the troopers organized, Easy approached the first bridge at the Wilhelmina Canal. Aware of the threat the Allied troops posed, the Germans exploded the bridge, raining wood, dirt and stone on the men. Easy camped for the night as British engineers built a temporary bridge.

Easy finally entered Eindhoven and was joyously welcomed by the jubilant citizens who offered food and drinks to the men who had rescued them from four years of German occupation. There were smiles, dancing and handshakes, hugs and pats on the backs. The men posed for photographs and obliged when asked for their autographs. Finally, the Dutch could proudly wave their orange flags (representing their national color) in public without fear of retribution from the Germans. The good times would soon end.

Fulfilling their obligations required Easy pushed through the crowds and secure the other bridges. Easy Company fought in close combat with the Germans in Nuenen. Fifteen casualties forced Easy Company to admit its first retreat — back into Eindhoven. Easy Company was just beginning 72 days of combat, and more loss.

THE ISLAND – "FIX BAYONETS"

Still in The Netherlands on October 2nd, the 506th was the first unit of the 101st Airborne to cross the bridge at Nijmagen and move into "The Island," a flat and agricultural area of land about three miles across, below sea level, requiring dikes (levees) over 20 feet high to hold back the water.

Sparsely numbered along the front lines, a nighttime Easy Company patrol came upon a group of elite German SS troops. A quick and intense combat ensued between the forces on each side of the dike. Private James "Moe" Alley was injured by a grenade, causing 32 wounds to his face, neck and arm. Shrapnel from a grenade damaged the radio on Rod Strohl's back, preventing the patrol from calling for help. Looking at the overwhelming number of German troops, the small Easy Company patrol had no choice but to retreat and report their findings to Winters.

Winters organized a new patrol and still leading from the front, went ahead alone to scout the German forces. Devising a plan, he waited for more reinforcements to arrive. Winters had made a quick appraisal of the situation: the Germans had solid cover behind an elevated road, about 200 yards away. Easy Company was in a shallow ditch, in an open field, soon to be exposed by the morning sunlight. Easy was the only protection between the Germans and the 2nd Battalion HQ (headquarters) behind them. For Winters, the best option was to go on the offensive against the Germans.

Once the reinforcements arrived, Winters briefed his men and gave the order, "Fix bayonets." The command was a rare directive that caused the mens' hearts to race. Winters gave the command and a smoke grenade was thrown to silently give the signal to everyone waiting in the ditch. Time to charge! During the run, some of the men tripped on low, unseen barbed wire in the field. Not looking back during the sprint, Winters reached the top of the elevated road alone, where he saw one German soldier in front of him and a mass of German soldiers to his right. Surprised to be almost face to face with the enemy, Winters jumped back on his side of the elevated road. Both solitary combatants threw grenades, neither of which exploded, allowing Winters the opportunity to get back on the top of the road and shoot from the hip, eliminating the single German. Winters then opened fire on the large group of Germans, only 50 feet away, just as the rest of his men arrived. Combined with the placed machine guns and mortars, they began a concentrated gunfire on the retreating enemy. The Germans were routed.

Winters' planning and tactics, along with superior training and implementation by his troops, allowed Easy to beat a superior force of about 300 elite German SS troops with only 35 men. In all aspects of combat infantry strategy and maneuvers, Winters felt this victory, in the face of numerically superior enemy, was Easy Company's pinnacle achievement during the war.

This decisive melee was also the last time Winters would fire his weapon in combat. A few days later, Winters was promoted to second in command of the 2nd Battalion of the 506th. He would now assist in leading Dog, Easy and Fox companies.

Having been with Easy Company from the start of their journey, leaving his brothers was a difficult task for Winters; he had served, suffered, survived and succeeded alongside his men.

OPERATION *PEGASUS*

The failure of Operation *Market-Garden* left thousands of British soldiers trapped behind enemy lines in The Netherlands. A few hundred British soldiers were able to escape capture. Those soldiers were often kept in hiding by the Dutch resistance. The resistance was made up of ordinary citizens who conducted operations against the Germans such as: spying, sabotage and providing shelter for Jewish families and Allied aircrews and soldiers caught behind the German's lines.

After escaping as a prisoner and being on the run for four weeks, Lt. Colonel David Dobie of the British 1st Airborne Division swam across the Rhine River near Arnhem and made contact with Colonel Sink. Col. Dobie had become the leader of almost 140 men trying to get back to the Allied lines. Col. Sink put Easy Company commander, 1st Lt. Fred "Moose" Heylinger (who replaced Winters) in charge of the rescue, code named Operation *Pegasus*. Col. Dobie then swam back across the river to share the plot with his men and to be with them when the time came for it to unfold.

The night before the planned operation, collapsible boats were hidden on the riverbank by Canadian engineers. On the night of October 22nd, into the early hours of the next morning, twenty-four men from Easy Company paddled silently across the river. Meanwhile, on the other side of the river, the British used a flashlight to make the "V" for victory sign to inform Easy Company where to land the boats. Corporal Walter Gordon and Corporal Francis Mellett set up machine guns on the flank while Heylinger made contact with the British. To say the British were thrilled to see the "Yanks" (the British nickname for the Americans) was an enormous understatement! The British were so ecstatic that the Americans had to keep reminding them to be quiet so as to not alert the Germans.

With the ever-present threat of being discovered, the large group of the rescuers and the rescued safely paddled back to the American lines. The entire effort took about an hour and a half and was completed without any problems. The men of Easy Company were all given commendations. In celebration, Col. Dobie gave his troops a party.

Easy Company was finally relieved by Canadian soldiers after 72 days on the front line against the Germans in The Netherlands. During that time, none of the men had been able to take a shower. Trucks took them back to France for some rest, new uniforms…and finally, a hot shower. Once again, Easy Company gave all it had. The men endured wet and cold weather, wore the same clothes for months and did not have enough quality food.

The Netherlands campaign cost over 50 Easy Company men in the fighting.

BASTOGNE

Early in the morning on December 16, 1944, Hitler launched a large-scale attack of 200,000 men and 1,000 tanks in the forests of the Ardennes that caught the Allies completely by surprise. This attack was known as the "Battle of the Bulge" because the Germans would 'bulge' out the Allies' front lines at the town of Bastogne, Belgium. At this stage of the war, the Germans desperately needed to take and hold Bastogne because of the seven roads that led from the town made it a vital centralized location to keep their tanks and troops moving westward against the Allies. It became the largest battle ever fought by the U.S. Army.

The 101st Airborne was sent to Bastogne, and quickly the paratroopers became surrounded, again. This time, the men traveled into battle by trucks and called their deployment a "tail-gate" jump as they were jumping from the back of trucks rather than out of planes. The sudden and surprise attack imposed on Easy Company meant the men did not have time to collect basic winter clothes, much less gather enough ammunition. As Easy Company made its way toward its positions, they passed troops who had already bore the brunt of the German offensive. Lacking their own gear, Easy Company pilfered as much of the retreating soldiers' supplies as they could.

The winter was one of the worst in decades, and that proved to be as big an enemy as the Germans. Without proper boots and supplies of dry socks, the men suffered from frostbite and "trench foot," where a combination of wet and cold feet caused circulation and infection problems. Close to one-third of all the injuries were related to the severe weather conditions. With no hot food, little sleep, the stress of combat and never being able to get warm, the men lived in a constant state of extreme fatigue for almost two weeks, sometimes pushing them to the breaking point. However, a trip off the line for a couple days to be assigned as a runner at the command post often rejuvenated a man enough to allow him to return to the front lines.

German artillery exploded at the tree-top level and sent metal and wood shrapnel raining down on the men in foxholes. Sometimes, the enemy firepower was set to explode on the ground, literally bouncing the men who lay in their foxholes. One such artillery barrage badly injured Joe Toye's leg while he was standing out in the open. "Wild" Bill Guarnere ran out to help his wounded buddy when the shelling stopped. Just at that moment, another artillery round landed, taking one of Guarnere's legs as well. But even hunkered down in a foxhole was no guarantee of safety. A direct hit on their foxhole killed "Skip" Muck and Alex Penkala. All four of these men were experienced and beloved members of the company. Their losses were crushing.

Because the wounded could only be moved off the front lines back into town, the 101st turned a church into a makeshift hospital. Lacking supplies and with little hope of getting a new inventory meant bandages had to be boiled in water and reused. The town, like its surrounding countryside, continued to be subjected to German artillery barrages. Being surrounded meant there was no place to escape the fighting; nowhere to run, nowhere to hide and no rest for the weary men.

On December 22nd, the Germans delivered a message to General McAuliffe, the acting 101st Airborne commander, demanding the surrender of the Americans. The General's reply was, "Nuts!" This declaration was a decisively negative response to the suggestion that the proud and determined 101st Airborne would ever give up. To this day, the citizens of Bastogne celebrate this famous rebuttal by throwing chestnuts to the crowd from the balcony of city hall.

Eventually, the weather cleared enough for C-47s to air drop supplies, a most-welcome sight for the fatigued troops. The day after Christmas, tanks from General Patton's 3rd Army breached the German's lines, allowing more supplies to be brought in and the wounded to be finally evacuated to hospitals. The 101st Airborne's determined defense of Bastogne earned them the Distinguished Unit Citation for the second time.

The hostilities at Bastogne extracted a terrible toll on all who fought there. The Allies suffered over 70,000 causalities, but the Germans lost even more. All the men would say they never, _ever_ want to be as cold as they were in Bastogne...and being proud paratroopers, they also said they did not need to be rescued by General Patton!

Foy - Medics

Sitting in their foxholes in the Bois Jacques (Jack's Woods), Easy Company had been looking down the hill on the village of Foy, Belgium, during the Battle of the Bulge. At this time, Easy's leader was now Lt. Norman Dike. Orders from Division HQ selected 2nd Battalion of the 506th to carry out the attack on Foy. It was time to move forward, out of the woods. On January 13, 1945, Easy Company was tasked with leading the attack; the Germans were watching and waiting. For a second time, Easy Company had to run across 250 yards of open field, a terrible disadvantage for them against the German troops already entrenched in houses in the village.

As a battalion commander, Winters watched from the tree line as Easy kicked off the attack and the Germans began shooting and launching heavy artillery. In the middle of the run, Lt. Dike froze. Just like in Carentan, sitting there would only get the men shot! Lt. Dike, however, was no Winters, who had courageously jumped into the line of fire at Carentan to save his men. Winters wanted to run into the field and take over, but his new Battalion command position required him to delegate orders. 1st Lt. Ronald Speirs, a platoon leader in Dog Company, was close-by. Winters ordered Speirs to take over the attack. Speirs instantly obeyed the order and ran into the field of heavy incoming fire. With his decisive leadership, Easy Company resumed its charge into Foy, clearing it of German occupation. Lt. Dike was relieved of command. Easy Company was now in Speirs' capable hands where he would remain as its leader for the duration of the war.

Don Malarkey was commanding the 2nd Platoon mortar squad and remained at the Bois Jacques with his mortar teams for their role in the battle. From up on a hill, he could easily see 1st and 2nd Platoons charging toward Foy, as well as 3rd Platoon's diversionary attack, aimed at confusing the Germans. Casualties quickly mounted as the men closed in on the village. Malarkey later recalled, with a combination of awe and pride, witnessing the strategy play out: "During the attack on Foy, I could see 3rd Platoon, hung up in that orchard, taking casualties, and plain as day, watched medic Gene Roe run across a field of open ground and begin treating those men." Malarkey went on to say that despite the incoming fire, Roe continued to dart from man to man, applying first aid and telling each that he would make it, no matter how grievous the wounds.

Later on, Malarkey spoke with medic Doc Roe about Roe's lack of awards. Like many of the men who served with Roe and gave witness to his heroics – some of whom only survived the war because of his heroics -- Malarkey believed Roe earned and deserved far more medals for bravery than he was ever awarded. Looking slightly embarrassed over the question, Roe humbly said that he "didn't do anything special and was proud of what he did have." Malarkey was adamant when the subject of Eugene Roe came up: "He was a phenomenal combat medic." Even though Roe was nominated for the Silver Star by Lt. Jack Foley, for an unknown reason he was never awarded the commendation.

While Eugene Roe was the only medic from Easy to make it from D-Day to the Eagle's Nest, medics Ed Pepping, Al Mampre, Ralph Spina and Earnest Oats (who died on D-Day in the Stick #66 crash) all served with distinction. Medics were special soldiers in every aspect. Because they were not allowed to carry a weapon, they could not defend themselves, nor fight back. And so, the other guys watched over them and protected them. When the battle began, every soldier was trying to find cover from the bullets and the bombs. But the cry of "Medic!" brought that soldier wearing the red cross armband running toward the wounded, at his own peril, to provide medical attention and comfort.

Several Easy Company men referred to the medics as "angels."

GERMANS IN RETREAT

In mid-April, 1945, not long after pushing into Germany, the 101st Airborne quartermaster delivered one pair of socks and three bottles of Coca-Cola to each man. It was most definitely a cause for celebration, obtaining what was considered everyday comforts back home!

Due to the Allies' aerial bombardment, much of Germany's railways had been destroyed. Just to get into Germany, Easy's train ride had to detour through Holland, Belgium, Luxembourg and France where Easy then boarded transport trucks and moved through the German interior, crossing the Rhine and Danube Rivers. Many of the small towns and villages along the route had escaped the ravages of war. Thus, when it was time for the convoy to stop for the night, the soldiers told the German residents they had 30 minutes to leave their homes. How the men enjoyed sleeping under real roofs, in real beds and under real sheets, especially since those beds had recently been vacated by the enemy! There was little sympathy offered by the American soldiers, who had witnessed so many destroyed homes in the countries Germany had invaded.

Passing deeper into Germany, Easy began to see small groups of German soldiers surrendering. Those smaller groups soon grew into larger groups as Easy reached the Autobahn (highway), now solely reserved for the Allies driving east into the heart of Germany. With no civilian vehicles allowed on the highway, the wide, grassy median between the roads and the shoulders were used by surrendering German troops marching west into awaiting POW (prisoner of war) camps. As far as the men's eyes could see, the German troops marched in full uniform. Many still had their weapons since there had been no time to disarm them. Amazing as it sounds, sometimes only a handful of American troops guarded hundreds of Germans in open fields.

The masses of grey uniforms trudging resolutely down the grassy passageway meant the end of the German Army. There would not be another surprise attack like Bastogne. The will to fight had left the German Army. Munich fell to the American 7th Army, an important city for the Nazis. But Easy didn't care about capturing Munich; for them the race was for the ultimate prized location high in the Alps.

But first, Easy Company would see firsthand, the evil of the Nazi regime.

CONCENTRATION CAMP

On April 29th, Easy Company stopped for the night near Landsberg, Germany. Patrols were sent out, always looking for any remaining resistance by German troops. Sergeant Frank Perconte reported back to Winters that his patrol had found a camp containing more than 5,000 people. Winters arrived in his jeep with Captain Lewis Nixon and found men, half-starved and emaciated, lined up along the barbed wire-fence, many wearing blue-and-white-striped clothing. The large camp consisted of small huts that were halfway dug in the ground and so short in height that prisoners had to bend over in order to walk inside them. This was a work camp and part of the larger Dachau camp system.

The smell was atrocious! The living conditions were appalling. Those who had died were left lying on the ground in the camp or stacked in piles as no attempt had been made to bury them or care for their remains. When word of the approaching American forces reached the Germans, almost all the camp's guards fled.

Winters made radio contact with Col. Sink to inform him of the discovery. By the time Col. Sink arrived, Private Joe Liebgott, who spoke some German, had been able to translate enough to understand the camp was mostly for Jews.

Without another thought, Winters hurriedly ordered cheese from the nearby town to be brought and fed to the prisoners. But Major Kent, the 506th doctor, arrived and told Winters to stop handing out food. Due to the advanced state of malnutrition, the prisoners had to be given food under the careful watch of medical personnel. Too much food, too fast, was almost as dangerous to their health as not having any food at all. Delivering the news to the weakened survivors that the food had to be taken away was an agonizing and disheartening task for the young Liebgott.

General Taylor brought in the news media to record and document the atrocities and ordered the civilians living nearby to help clean the camp, and bare-handed bury the dead. This was meant as punishment and also, as a lesson for those who had inflicted so much horror on so many innocent people. Such penance would ensure that the German people could not claim to be unaware of the actions done in their name.

The sights and smells would be forever emblazoned in the memory of the men of Easy Company, reinforcing what they already knew: their fight was crucial, and it was much bigger than just themselves!

BERCHTESGADEN/EAGLE'S NEST

Orders had come from high up that the 101st was to be awarded first entrance into Berchtesgaden. When Colonel Sink told Major Winters to prepare the men for the trip, the Major was elated. While it was just a small town in a deep valley on the Germany/Austria border, Berchtesgaden was well-known to the men. Numerous photos of Hitler meeting with the leaders of England, Italy and France in Berchtesgaden had been widely publicized in the newspapers and magazines. Besides capturing Berlin, Berchtesgaden and the Eagle's Nest were the next most treasured locations. Soldiers and generals from all the Allied armies knew they would be forever immortalized if they were the first to seize this site. The French 2nd Armored Division was also in the area and wanted to raise the French flag as revenge for the years of occupation; thus, the Americans had to hasten their advance.

On the mountain route, blown bridges caused Easy Company to have to back-track a couple of times in order to find an alternative path that would allow them to be the first to gain entrance into the infamous location. Easy finally reached Berchtesgaden on May 5, 1945. While some troops from the U.S. and France had been in the town and left, there were very few indications that the 101st Airborne was not the first to arrive. Easy dutifully secured the hotel, Berchtesgaden Hof, for General Taylor. Winters and Lt. Welsh made themselves at home by sharing a large box of Hitler's silverware.

A short drive up the steep road from there led to Obersalzberg, a private, village-like retreat that boasted homes for Hitler and the very top ranking Nazis, along with barracks for elite SS soldiers who served as guards for the compound. Hitler had spent more time here than anywhere else during his time in power. Winters and Lt. Nixon found a railroad car full of stolen artwork from all across Europe. The soldiers had a field day driving Hitler's staff cars and making sure the cars' windows were really bulletproof. They discovered German uniforms and posed for comical photos while wearing the newly acquired clothing. There were plenty of souvenirs to be had for everyone!

Further up the mountain was Hitler's Eagle's Nest at 6,100 feet. It was a guest house at the top of the mountain; a gift to Hitler for his 50th birthday. The only way to reach the Eagle's Nest was through a tunnel into the mountain that led to an elevator whose walls were polished brass, with a mirrored finish that looked like gold. Alton More found a photo album of Hitler with many high ranking German officials who had visited the Eagle's Nest. More had to hide the album in the seat cushion of his jeep in order to keep it away from an officer who wanted it for himself.

Word soon came: "Effective immediately, all troops will stand fast on present positions. German Army Group G in this sector has surrendered. No firing on Germans unless fired upon." For any soldier, Easy's "present position" was about as good as it could get.

Easy Company had reached the summit of the mountain and the pinnacle of Hitler's residences in his Nazi regime. The beautiful scenery allowed a peaceful duty the men could not have imagined during the months of war. On May 7, Easy Company received news that the German Army had surrendered! Finally, the men could truly relax, and relax they did. Every night brought drinking from bottles that had once, not too long ago, belonged to Hitler and Herman Goering, the commander of the German air force.

As a *coup de grâce*, they raised their glasses while sitting in the same spots they had seen in the newspapers and magazine, just as Hitler once did.

KAPRUN/WAR'S END

The war in Europe officially ended on May 8, 1945. The men of Easy Company then loaded into trucks and traveled to Kaprun, Austria, about 20 miles (30 km) away from Berchtesgaden. The men continued to be overwhelmed by the beauty of the landscape, which looked like something out of a picture book. The tranquil and picturesque Alps afforded an opportunity for them to recall what life was like without war.

Part of the duties of the 2nd Battalion (only 600 men) was to guard 25,000 German prisoners of war (POWs). The men also went out on patrols to locate any stragglers from the German Army and brought them to the POW camps. Any SS troops discovered were sent to Nuremberg, Germany. By now, documentation was accumulating that proved the SS troops had carried out many acts of evil and carnage on behalf of the Nazi name and they would now face charges of war crimes.

Another major issue were the thousands of civilians who were displaced persons (DPs). They were from Poland, Hungary, Czechoslovakia, Belgium, The Netherlands and France. Eventually, both the enemy soldiers and DPs were sorted out and taken out of the area.

In their spare time, the men were able to enjoy sporting events and competitions between units. Tennis courts were set up, as well as rifle ranges to keep up the mens' skills. They could go hunting for goats in the mountains. They could ride a ski lift up to a mountain lodge and spend a few days at a time relaxing and taking on the slopes. The clear, calm lake at Zell Am See allowed for casual boating and a parachute jump right into the water. The men also enjoyed a true taste of home, baseball games.

Getting out of the Army and going home was the priority of almost every man. A points system was established based on certain criteria: the number of months of service, the number of months overseas, the number of medals received and the number of children back home. For a soldier to receive his discharge papers, he had to have a total of 85 points. It was at times, a very unfair system. Earl McClung was one of Easy's best soldiers and had volunteered to lead countless dangerous patrols. McClung had been on the front lines the entire war and yet, still lacked the 85 points required. He and many others would have to wait several more months to finally go home.

Easy Company had come a long way, literally and figuratively. From Sobel to Winters to Speirs and from Toccoa to Normandy to Kaprun; it had taken almost three years. In that time, their singular bond had driven them to risk punishment from the Army for going absent without leave (AWOL) from the hospitals, without being fully recovered and healed, just so they could return to be with their buddies. Strohl, Wynn, Alley, Welsh and Toye (still with his arm in a sling) all had gone AWOL at some point in the war just to avoid being sent to another unit. Time in Kaprun allowed each man to reflect on his friends around him, and too, his friends who were not there.

By July 1945, the high-point Toccoa men were finally enroute back to the States. Japan surrendered on August 14, 1945. On November 30, 1945, the 101st Airborne was deactivated. On paper, Easy Company no longer existed.

Their country had called and they responded willingly and without hesitation. They volunteered to fight alongside the best, with a guarantee to be surrounded by the enemy. They entered the United States Army as ordinary civilians, and became elite paratroopers. Strangers had become brothers. However, once many of the men returned to civilian life, they struggled. Surrounded by their families again, some found they could not reconnect. Even if they wanted to talk about what they had done in the war and what they had seen, they could not find the words. How could they burden their loved ones with some of their memories? For many of the men, those memories haunted them in their dreams. In a strange sort of way, some longed to be back with their brothers where they did not need to explain themselves to the guy next to them. It would take time to become civilians again.

Part of them would always remain a soldier in Easy Company.

CROSSES

By the end of the war, 366 men had served in Easy Company. Of those, 47 had paid the ultimate price for our freedom; they would never enjoy the peace at war's end. Nor would they come home to their parents, siblings and friends for that first heartfelt, emotional embrace. Their sacrifices had cost them not only their lives, but it also cost them their dreams, hopes and aspirations that all young people yearn to accomplish.

Several Easy Company soldiers still lie at rest under crosses in the cemeteries in Normandy, The Netherlands, Luxemburg and Belgium. They join more than 45,000 other men who died to save the world from tyranny and evil, still buried in the foreign soil on which they fought.

The cemeteries are a sight to see. The grounds are immaculate. Every tree and every bush is constantly trimmed. The grass is always cut and edged. Meticulous care is taken to assure each cross and Star of David is perfectly aligned in height and in rows, no matter the angle from which they are viewed. Visitors walk in silence, in awe and in reverence. The crosses stand as quiet and somber reminders of the high cost of freedom – and freedom is never free.

Bill Guarnere and Joe Toye (whom everyone felt was the strongest guy in Easy Company) both returned home with only one leg. Ed Tipper lost an eye. Max Meth lost a hand. Many bore the physical scars from combat injuries on their bodies; almost everyone bore scars internally. The war would change them all forever. Even as they aged into their 80s and 90s, they all said not a day goes by that they do not think of the men they served with in Easy Company. They never could forget the men who became their brothers. Theirs is a bond completely unique in human nature; one founded on total dependence on each other as combat infantry soldiers.

The men of Easy Company gathered for a reunion every year from 1947 to 2012, as a testament to that bond and to their life-long brotherhood… and every year they toasted the men who were buried beneath those crosses on distant soil.

Theirs is a story of humility, courage, honor, sacrifice, duty and patriotism. We, too, can never forget!

HONOR ROLL

EASY COMPANY MEN WHO WERE KILLED IN ACTION (KIA)
* denotes former Easy Company men KIA with other units

Rudolph R. Dittrich	5·20·1944	James L. Diel*	9·19·1944
Robert J. Bloser	6·6·1944	Vernon J. Menze	9·20·1944
Herman F. Collins	6·6·1944	James W. Miller	9·20·1944
George L. Elliot	6·6·1944	William T. Miller	9·20·1944
William S. Evans	6·6·1944	Robert Van Klinken	9·20·1944
Joseph M. Jordan	6·6·1944	Raymond G. Schmitz*	9·22·1944
Robert L. Matthews	6·6·1944	James Campbell	10·5·1944
William McGonigal, Jr.	6·6·1944	William Dukeman, Jr.	10·5·1944
Thomas Meehan	6·6·1944	John T. Julian	12·21·1944
William S. Metzler	6·6·1944	Donald B. Hoobler	1·3·1945
John N. Miller	6·6·1944	Richard F. Hughes	1·9·1945
Sergio G. Moya	6·6·1944	Warren H. Muck	1·10·1945
Elmer L. Murray, Jr.	6·6·1944	Alex M. Penkala, Jr.	1·10·1945
Ernest L. Oats (medic)	6·6·1944	Harold B. Webb	1·10·1945
Richard E. Owen	6·6·1944	A. P. Herron	1·13·1945
Carl N. Riggs	6·6·1944	Francis J. Mellett	1·13·1945
Murray B. Roberts	6·6·1944	Patrick Neill	1·13·1945
Gerald R. Snider	6·6·1944	Carl C. Sowosko	1·13·1945
Elmer L. Telstad	6·6·1944	John E. Shindell	1·13·1945
Thomas W. Warren	6·6·1944	Kenneth J. Webb	1·13·1945
Jerry A. Wentzel	6·6·1944	William F. Kiehn	2·10·1945
Ralph H. Wimer	6·6·1944	Eugene E. Jackson	2·10·1945
Benjamin J. Stoney*	6·7·1944	John A. Janovec	5·16·1945
Terrence C. Harris*	6·13·1944		

BAND OF BROTHERS FAMILY FOUNDATION

The Band of Brothers Family Foundation is an IRS 501c3 organization (EIN 81-2710879) that was established by the descendants of the men of Easy Company, 506th Parachute Infantry Regiment, 101st Airborne, WWII. The board and body of the Foundation are made up solely by family members.

Our primary goal is to educate students on the men of Easy Company (our heroes) and on WWII in general. We hope to place this book in the hands of as many students and school libraries as possible. We, Continue to Honor.

If you know a school library or a school teacher who would benefit from having this book, please let us know.

https://www.facebook.com/Band of Brothers Family Foundation

easycofoundation@gmail.com

Books Referenced and Further Reading

- Band of Brothers by Stephen Ambrose
- Beyond Band of Brothers by Major Dick Winters and Col. (Ret.) Cole G. Kingseed
- Conversations with Major Dick Winters by Col. (Ret.) Cole G. Kingseed
- Call of Duty by Lynn "Buck" Compton with Marcus Brotherton
- Easy Company Soldier by Don Malarkey with Bob Welsh (page 52 quoted on March to Atlanta & page 115 quoted on Laundry)
- Shifty's War by Marcus Brotherton
- Parachute Infantry by David Webster
- Brothers in Arms, Best of Friends by Bill Guarnere and Edward Heffron with Robyn Post
- Silver Eagle by Clancy Lyall and Ronald Ooms
- Biggest Brother: The Life of Major Dick Winters by Larry Alexander
- A Company of Heroes by Marcus Brotherton
- We Who are Alive and Remain by Marcus Brotherton
- Fighting with the Screaming Eagles by Robert Bowen
- The Filthy Thirteen by Richard Killblane and Jake McNiece
- Fighting Fox Company, The Battling Flank of the Band of Brothers by Terry Poyser with Bill Brown
- D-Day with the Screaming Eagles by George Koskimaki (and others by the author)
- Vanguard of the Crusade by Mark Bando (and others by the author)
- The Simple Sounds of Freedom by Thomas H. Taylor
- Tonight We Die as Men by Ian Gardner (and others by the author)
- Nuts! A 101st Airborne Machine Gunner at Bastogne by Vincent Speranza
- Look Out Below! A story of the Airborne by a Paratrooper Padre by Francis L. Sampson

Chris Langlois is a grandson of medic Eugene Gilbert Roe, Sr. Roe joined Easy Company at Camp Mackall, just after Toccoa. Chris is originally from Baton Rouge, Louisiana and graduated from Louisiana State University. He currently resides in Dallas, Texas with his wife, Patricia, and daughter, Julia. Both Chris and Patricia are police officers. Chris is donating a portion of the profits to the Band of Brothers Family Foundation, so more copies of this book can be placed in school libraries and classrooms. He started Doc Roe Publishing (on Facebook, Instagram and Twitter). Chris can be reached at: docroegrandson@gmail.com

Anneke Helleman is from the Netherlands where she lives with her husband Gert-Jan IJzerman. She has a son and a daughter, both of whom are happily married. She is also a proud grandmother. She is co-owner of a furniture shop and a professional painter. Her artwork stretches from Realism to hand lettering WWII Aircraft Nose-Art on leather jackets. Her passion for WWII began when she visited the American Cemetery in Margraten and heard stories of some of the soldiers buried there. She is forever grateful for her freedom.
Anneke can be reached at: info@annekehelleman.nl

CPSIA information can be obtained at www.ICGtesting.com
Printed in the USA
LVIW01n1641050318
568696LV00015B/266